HIPPO BOOKS No. 7

£ 0·25
U.K. PRICE

Dogs

by Edmund Burke

HAMLYN
LONDON · NEW YORK · SYDNEY · TORONTO

Breed: AFGHAN HOUND

ORIGIN Asia (Near East, Afghanistan, India, Persia).

SIZE
Dogs—27–29 inches at shoulder, to 65 pounds.
Bitches—25–27 inches at shoulder, to 55 pounds.

COLOUR
Mostly colours range from cream through a rich golden red. Black-and-tans are also known. Whites or white markings are penalised at exhibitions.

COAT
Thick, fine textured silky hair covers the legs, fore-quarters, ribs, flanks and hind-quarters. Ears and feet well feathered. In the mature dogs there is a long saddle of short hair along the back from the shoulders. This is a necessary point in the dog's conformation.

SPECIAL CHARACTERISTICS
The tail, which is set fairly low, should curve into a ring at the end but must never be carried over the back, nor be bushy. The hair on the head, from the forehead back grows into a distinctive top-knot.

USES
A hunting dog in its native lands, the Afghan Hound is primarily a member of the greyhound family, hunts by sight, is swift and well adapted to travel over poor terrain.

HISTORY
Claimed by many to be the oldest breed of dog in the world with a legendary past stretching back to the Ark. First introduced in Britain about 1907.

Breed: **AIREDALE TERRIER**

ORIGIN   Great Britain (England).

SIZE
Dogs—23–24 inches at the shoulder, 45–50 pounds.
Bitches—22–23 inches at the shoulder, 40–45 pounds.

COLOUR
Head and ear dark, rich tan, legs, chest and under parts of the body also
tan. Black or grizzled saddle. A white blaze on the chest is sometimes seen.

COAT
Wiry, dense and hard, lying close to the body. Soft undercoat.

SPECIAL CHARACTERISTICS
The largest British terrier, the Airedale is a sturdy working dog, with a
longish head free from wrinkles. The ears are V-shaped, set on the side
of the head. If the ear is folded the top line should be above the level of
the skull. The eyes are small and dark, giving an indication of spirit,
alertness and intelligence. Yellow eyes should not occur.

USES
Bred as a vermin hunter, equally at ease on land or in water, the Airedale
has taken its place among the real working dogs of the world. The breed
was used, with great success, in the armed forces in the First World War.

HISTORY
The basic stock from which British Airedale Terriers derive is the now
vanished Waterside Terrier. The Otterhound also played a part in the
formation of the breed as did the Bull Terrier.

Breed: **ALSATIAN (German Shepherd Dog)**

ORIGIN Germany (Thuringia).

SIZE
Dogs—24–26 inches at the shoulder.
Bitches—22–24 inches at the shoulder.
Weight to 125 pounds.

COLOUR
Any colour other than pure white is allowed at exhibitions.

COAT
Double coated, with the undercoat dense and woolly. The hard outer-coat is flat and rain resistant.

SPECIAL CHARACTERISTICS
Alert, fearless, faithful, vigilant. Each dog is an individual with a high standard of intelligence.

USES
Developed by crossing various German pastoral breeds, the Alsatian is primarily a working dog. Classified as ' Non-Sporting ', it is best known for its work with the police and armed forces.

HISTORY
The breed came into being largely as the result of the work of a German cavalry officer, Rittmeister von Stephanitz. Alsatians gained world fame through two dogs, Strongheart and Rin-Tin-Tin, both of whom were early canine film stars.

Breed: **BASENJI**

ORIGIN   Africa (The Congo regions).

SIZE
    Dogs—17 inches at shoulder.
    Bitches—16 inches at shoulder.

COLOUR
    Chestnut or fawn with white points, black-and-white or black-and-tan-and-white.

COAT
    A short very silky coat set close to an extremely pliable skin.

SPECIAL CHARACTERISTICS
    Head is of medium width, tapers towards the eyes. The ' stop ', or line from skull to nose is ' broken ' or definite. The nose should be black. The ears are pointed and erect, giving a wrinkle to the skin between. The eyes are a dark hazel, almond-shaped, deep-set. The tail is set very high, must be carried in a tight curl at one side. The breed does not bark but is capable of a peculiar yodelling sound.

USES
    Primarily a show dog and pet, the Basenji has been trained as a retriever.

HISTORY
    Undoubtedly an ancient breed, the Basenji is reputed to have existed in Classical Egypt but was lost to the later world. During the last century travellers in Africa saw the dogs hunting with the natives and began to bring them out to the rest of the world. The first pair were imported to Britain in 1895 but the breed did not really become established until 1937.

Breed: **BASSET HOUND**

ORIGIN   France.

SIZE
    Dogs—13 inches at the shoulder, 50 pounds.
    Bitches—12 inches at the shoulder, 45 pounds.

COLOUR
    Any hound colour is acceptable, although among the combinations more often seen are black-and-tan, tri-colours (black-and-white-and-tan) black and-whites and lemon-and-whites.

COAT
    Medium texture, lying close to the skin—neither too coarse nor too fine but of sufficient strength to protect the dog in thick cover.

SPECIAL CHARACTERISTICS
    The head is large, the skull tending to narrowness and length. The head should resemble that of the Bloodhound. The skin on the head is loose so that when a dog leans forward to put its nose to the ground the skin on head and cheeks falls forward and wrinkles. Legs are extremely short and heavily boned and the feet appear splayed. Ears are long enough so that when drawn forward they should cover the nose easily.

USES
    As an overall hunting dog, with an exceptionally keen nose.

HISTORY
    Developed in France and Belgium, the Basset Hound was first introduced into Britain in 1866.

Breed: **BEAGLE**

ORIGIN Not definitely known, but presumably England.

SIZE
Should not exceed 16 inches at the shoulder.
Many Beagles are well under this height.

COLOUR
Any colour or mixture of colours which presents the true appearance of a hound is permissible at an exhibition.

COAT
Medium-length coat which is close and hard.

SPECIAL CHARACTERISTICS
The Beagle is in appearance a miniature of the Foxhound. He must however look big for his size and give the appearance of being able to follow his quarry anywhere. The eyes are large, set wide apart and have the gentle pleading look associated with hounds.

USES
Used in Great Britain mainly on hare, although formerly they were widely used on rabbit. Abroad they have made their name as an all-round hound working on fox, deer, squirrel and upland game birds.

HISTORY
The breed was well known and widely used in Britain before the time of the first Queen Elizabeth. She is reported to have favoured a 'pocket' Beagle, one with an average height of ten inches. Early records indicate that the breed resulted from the crossing of Foxhounds with Harriers and in some instances Beagles were called 'small' or 'little' Harriers.

Breed: **BEDLINGTON TERRIER**

ORIGIN   Great Britain (England).

SIZE
   15–16 inches at the shoulder, 22–24 pounds.

COLOUR
   Blue, blue and tan, liver, liver and tan.

COAT
   Unlike any other terrier, the Bedlington carries a soft, linty coat, not ov
   an inch in length, when in show condition.   It also carries a top-kno
   something shared only with the Dandie Dinmount.

SPECIAL CHARACTERISTICS
   There is no ' stop ' on the Bedlington head, that is the line from the sk
   to the nose is unbroken.   The ideal eye appears to be triangular in sha
   well sunk in the head.   The ears which hang along the sides of the he
   should carry a silky fringe at their tips. The neck is long, tapering a
   arched.

USES
   Like almost all terriers the Bedlington was developed to suit local con
   tions but is now an increasingly popular show dog.   They, should, howeve
   retain their ability to catch vermin.

HISTORY
   Early records of the breed show one dog which was listed both as
   Bedlington Terrier and a Dandie Dinmount.   It is possible, however, th
   Whippet blood was added at a later date to give the Bedlington i
   distinctive outline.

16

Breed: **BORDER TERRIER**

ORIGIN   Great Britain (England and Scotland).

SIZE
  Dogs—13–15½ pounds.
  Bitches—11½–14 pounds.

COLOUR
  Red, wheaten, blue-and-tan or grizzle-and-tan.

COAT
  Dense, hard to the touch, with a soft undercoat.

SPECIAL CHARACTERISTICS
  The Border Terrier has a head shaped like that of an otter, quite broad across the top of the skull with a short and strong muzzle. Ears are V-shaped, moderately thick and dropping slightly forward along the cheek.

USES
  Today, the Border Terrier hunts small game and vermin but in the early history of the breed, it was used on badger, otter and fox. Its keenness and compactness, combined with an excellent temperament make it a good house dog.

HISTORY
  A native of the Cheviot Hills, the Border Terrier was like so many British native breeds created to suit local conditions. They had to follow a horse for hours and still have enough stamina to tackle any game put up. The breed was not recognised by the Kennel Club until 1920 but it seems that they existed, or at least their prototypes did, as long ago as the seventeenth century.

Breed: **BOSTON TERRIER**

ORIGIN United States.

SIZE
Should not exceed 25 pounds in weight, broken into three classes:
Lightweight under 15 pounds.
Middleweight 15–20 pounds.
Heavyweight 20–25 pounds.

COLOUR
Brindle with white markings, although black with white markings is allowed at an exhibition.

COAT
Fine textured, short, smooth to the touch. A long coat or a coarse coat is considered poor.

SPECIAL CHARACTERISTICS
The Boston Terrier carries a square, flat skull, ideally free from wrinkle. Their ears are carried erect as are their naturally short tails. The breed is noted for its intelligence, which shows in the dark, round, wide-set eyes.

USES
As a pet and a show dog.

HISTORY
The Boston Terrier is one of the few American breeds. The foundation stock was imported from England in the form of the old Bull-and-Terrier. Used for pit fighting, the type gradually developed in and around the city of Boston. It is probable that French Bulldog blood was added to make the Boston Terrier as we know it today.

Breed: **BOXER**

ORIGIN Germany.

SIZE
Dogs—22–24 inches at the shoulder, 66 pounds.
Bitches—21–23 inches at the shoulder, 62 pounds.

COLOUR
Fawn and brindle. In the fawns the colour ranges from a light yellow
to a dark red. In brindles the black stripes are set on a yellow or red
brown background. A black mask on either is essential. White marking
do not disqualify the dog at exhibitions, providing that they do not cover
more than one-third of the total.

COAT
Short, lying smoothly against the body. In a bright light it should shine.

SPECIAL CHARACTERISTICS
A squarish dog, strong limbed and giving the impression of power and
sturdiness. Musculation is clear and powerfully developed. Although giving
the idea of speed, the Boxer must never be racily built. The ideal is well
proportioned and elegant without sacrificing any sturdiness.

USES
Derived from fighting and sporting dogs, the Boxer is essentially a worker
Although it is extremely popular everywhere as a 'Non-Sporting' animal
Is often seen in the United States guiding the blind.

HISTORY
The exact origin of the breed is unknown although many people think
that it is a result of crossing the Great Dane with the Bulldog.

Breed: **BULLDOG**

ORIGIN   Great Britain (England).

SIZE
Dogs—55 pounds.
Bitches—50 pounds.

COLOUR
Brindle, red, fawn, white, pied—with, preferably a black mask and muzzle

COAT
Fine-textured coat lying close.   Short and smooth to the touch.

SPECIAL CHARACTERISTICS
Massively powerful, set low to the ground and with a steady, determined
gait.   The head is the most striking feature of the breed, the ideal dog
having a skull the circumference of which should equal its own height
at the shoulder.

USES
The Bulldog today is valued purely as a pet and show specimen.   Tenacious
they are nonetheless gentle, even-tempered dogs.   Unfortunately, although
they might be said to be the 'British breed' they are becoming increasingly
rare.

HISTORY
One of the oldest of the British dogs, Bulldogs appear to descend directly
from the *pugnaces* of Roman times.   First called Bulldogs about 1600
they gained fame for their fighting spirit in bull-baiting.   Until that sport
was outlawed the breed found little social acceptance.

Breed: **BULL MASTIFF**

ORIGIN Great Britain (England).

SIZE
Dogs—25–27 inches at the shoulder, to 130 pounds.
Bitches—24–26 inches at the shoulder, to 110 pounds.

COLOUR
Brindle, fawn or red—any shade. A white blaze on the chest is permitted but is not considered desirable.

COAT
Lies flat on the body, being short, hard and weather resistant.

SPECIAL CHARACTERISTICS
A large, square skull, with some wrinkling. The stop is definite, the nose broad with nostrils spread. Eyes are dark or hazel, set wide. Ears are V-shaped, small and slightly darker in colour than body. Tail is set high, reaches down to the hocks, shows a marked taper, carried straight or curved, never high as with a hound.

USES
As a watch and guard dog.

HISTORY
Created by crossing the Bulldog with the Mastiff. Combines in theory the best qualities of both. Used by gamekeepers to stop poaching, they were recognised by the Kennel Club in 1925.

Breed: **BULL TERRIER**

ORIGIN   Great Britain (England).

SIZE
Up to 50 pounds. Anything under a weight of 25 pounds is considered a miniature.

COLOUR
Two distinct types are recognised :
White and coloured—including black and brindles, with white markings.

COAT
Flat, stiff to touch, short, dense, carries a fine gloss.

SPECIAL CHARACTERISTICS
The head is long, with little stop. The eyes are black, small and set so as to seem triangular. The tail is short and straight, set on low and tapers from where it joins the body to the tip. The feet are small, compact and cat-like, the gait springy.

USES
Predominantly as a pet and house guard. The Bull Terrier, however, did a great deal of military work during World War II.

HISTORY
The British Bull Terrier is the result of one man's campaign. Starting with the now extinct Bull-and-Terrier, James Hinks of Birmingham, crossed White English Terrier blood and that of the Dalmatian. From the resulting puppies he selected the whites and continued to breed from them until he achieved the dog he wanted, the white Bull Terrier.

Breed: **CAIRN TERRIER**

ORIGIN   Great Britain (Scotland).

SIZE
    Dogs—10 inches at the shoulder, 14 pounds.
    Bitches—9 inches at the shoulder, 13 pounds.

COLOUR
    Any colour except white. A dog with dark ears and muzzle is consider
    desirable.

COAT
    A weather-resistant and harsh outer coat, growing profusely. The und
    coat is short and soft, growing close to the body like fur.

SPECIAL CHARACTERISTICS
    A strong, free moving short-legged terrier, giving the appearance of gre
    activity and endurance. It should be deep ribbed and short coupled. T
    head short and wide is hairy and gives a foxy expression.

USES
    Like most terriers, the Cairn was bred for use with vermin including t
    wild cat of the Highlands. Today the Cairn is the most popular of t
    working terriers and makes an ideal dog for town as well as the country

HISTORY
    One of the oldest terriers in Britain, the Cairn was at one time known
    the Short-Haired Skye Terrier. King James I was said to have ha
    Cairn Terriers but they may only have been similar dogs. The bree
    existed early in the 19th century. Recognised by the Kennel Club in 191

Breed: **CAVALIER KING CHARLES SPANIEL**

ORIGIN   Great Britain (England).

SIZE
Approximately 14 pounds although considerable tolerance either way allowable.

COLOUR
Four colour variants are seen :
> Ruby—a rich, solid deep red.
> Blenheim—pearl-white background broken by chestnut markings.
> Tri-colour—Black-and-white with irregularly distributed tan marking
> Black-and-tan—Jet black with tan markings.

COAT
Long and silky.   Free from curl but with abundant feathering.

SPECIAL CHARACTERISTICS
The head is flat, the ears, which are long, set high.   The stop is extreme shallow, the muzzle tapers to a point.   The nostrils are large and blac Eyes are large, dark and round, tending to be rather prominent.   Th body is short, with a level back and well-developed ribs.

USES
As pets and companions or show dogs.

HISTORY
The breed derives its name from the fact that they were supposedly th favourites of Charles II.   In actual fact they had been court favourites early as the time of Charles I.

Breed: **CHIHUAHUA**

ORIGIN Mexico.

SIZE
8 pounds maximum, 2 pounds considered ideal.

COLOUR
Any colour or combination of colours is allowed at exhibitions although tan or beige is the most commonly seen.

COAT
Two types are recognised—the smooth-haired and the long-haired. In the smooth, which is the most popular, the hair is of extremely fine texture lying close to the skin and quite glossy. In the long-haired animals the coat may either be straight or slightly waved, with a ruff around the neck.

SPECIAL CHARACTERISTICS
Aside from its being the world's smallest dog there are two other features peculiar to the breed. The tail gives the appearance of flatness due to the fact that the hair is more profuse on either side, giving it a broad look.

USES
The Chihuahua is simply and solely a pet and companion. Although active and intelligent their size prevents them doing anything much more active than barking in alarm should the need arise.

HISTORY
According to legend these were the sacred dogs of the Aztec Indians of Mexico. Whether or not this is true the first of the tiny dogs seem to have been brought from the modern Mexican state of Chihuahua.

34

Breed: **CHOW CHOW**

ORIGIN China.

SIZE
Minimum height for the breed is 18 inches. It is more important that the dog is in proportion than that it is of a specific size.

COLOUR
Normal self-colours are red, black, blue, fawn, cream and white. The colours should be solid, without patchiness. Lighter shades on the backs of the thighs and the underside of the tail are permitted at exhibitions.

COAT
The Chow Chow has a dense, soft, woolly undercoat. The outer coat is thick, straight and stands out from the body. Outer coat most profuse on neck and chest giving a ruff in many cases.

SPECIAL CHARACTERISTICS
Broad, flat skull carrying little stop. Black nose is preferred but in blues and fawns the nose may be self coloured. The eyes are small, almond-shaped and dark. Ears are small, erect, set forward over the eyes. The tongue is blue as are the flews and the roof of the mouth.

USES
As a pet, companion and show dog.

HISTORY
The breed came from China where a certain amount of mystery surrounds its beginnings. Some Chinese records call it a mongrel but this is difficult to believe since it breeds true—that is, it transmits its own qualities and points to its progeny.

Breed: **COCKER SPANIEL**

ORIGIN   Great Britain (England).

SIZE
   Weight from 25–28 pounds.

COLOUR
   Black, red, golden, blue roan, black-and-white or tri-coloured.

COAT
   On the head the hair is short and fine but on the body it is longer, fla
   and silky in texture, often showing feathering.   There should be sufficier
   undercoat to give protection in the field but the coat should never be s
   long as to become a hindrance while working.

SPECIAL CHARACTERISTICS
   The most popular of all the sporting dogs, the Cocker Spaniel has foun
   favour for its size and its temperament.   Often known as the ' Merr
   Cocker ' it carries itself jauntily, should have a deep muzzle, soft mout
   and appealing eyes.   The ears, or leathers should be at least long enoug
   to reach the tip of the nose.

USES
   Although the Cocker Spaniel is primarily a sporting dog, working unde
   the gun, it is better known today as a companion.   The working type c
   Cocker is larger, tougher, sturdier than the show version of the breed.

HISTORY
   The Cocker, like all the Spaniels, derives from gun-dogs originally brough
   to Britain from the Continent of Europe.

Breed: **COLLIE (Rough)**

ORIGIN Great Britain (Scotland).

SIZE
Dogs—24 inches at the shoulder, about 60 pounds.
Bitches—22 inches at the shoulder, about 50 pounds.

COLOUR
Many colours are shown and allowed at exhibitions although the most popular are richly marked sables, black-and-tans and fawns.

COAT
Perhaps the most distinguishing feature of the breed. The outer coat is harsh to feel but the undercoat is so fine that in a good specimen it should be difficult to actually see the skin. The face and mask are smooth but the mane and frill are rich and thick. The front legs may be feathered but the hind legs should be smooth below the hock.

SPECIAL CHARACTERISTICS
An extremely lithe breed, with an alert character to their bearing and mien. No good collie ever carries excess weight.

USES
Bred as a working shepherd dog, the Rough Collie is now seen almost exclusively as a pet or show specimen.

HISTORY
Once a working animal in the Scottish highlands, the Rough Collie gained the favour of Queen Victoria and breeders set about remodelling it to conform to fashion.

Breed: **CORGI (Cardiganshire)**

ORIGIN Great Britain (Wales).

SIZE
10–12 inches at the shoulder.
Dogs to 24 pounds.
Bitches to 22 pounds.
Optimum length—36 inches.

COLOUR
Any colour, except pure white, is allowed at exhibitions.

COAT
Short or medium length of a dense quality, hard texture.

SPECIAL CHARACTERISTICS
Head is foxy, both in shape and appearance. Skull wide and flat, tapering towards the eyes. Nose is black. Eyes of medium size, preferably dark in colour. Ears rather large, set well back but normally carried erect. The tail is moderately long, set in line with the body. Under no circumstances should it be carried over the body.

USES
Like its cousin the Pembrokeshire Corgi, the Cardiganshire is primarily a cattle dog. As such it is still used in parts of its native Wales. Elsewhere it is a pet, companion or show dog.

HISTORY
Descended in all probability from the herd dogs of the Celts, the Corgi may also carry blood from the Swedish Valhund, introduced to Britain during the time of the great Viking raids.

Breed: **CORGI (Pembroke)**

ORIGIN   Great Britain (Wales).

SIZE
10–12 inches at the shoulder.
Dogs—20–24 pounds.
Bitches—18–22 pounds.

COLOUR
Red, Sable, Fawn, Black-and-Tan or Tricolour.   Either self-coloured or with white markings on neck, chest and legs.   A minimum amount of white is allowed on the head at exhibitions.

COAT
Medium-length coat distinguished by its density.   Wiry coats are not allowed at exhibitions.

SPECIAL CHARACTERISTICS
Bold looking dogs, giving an impression of intelligence, stamina and substance.   Quick moving, they are low to the ground, sturdy, alert and extremely active.

USES
Originally drovers' dogs, working the great herds which moved from pasture to market.   Probably one of the oldest British breeds, it is thought to have been introduced by Celtic herdsmen in prehistoric times.

HISTORY
Brave dogs, the Corgis not only served as drovers, helping in driving, but defended their masters against foot-pads and highwaymen.

Breed: **DACHSHUND (Standard and Miniature)**

ORIGIN Germany.

SIZE
Standard—Dogs 25 pounds, Bitches 23 pounds.
Miniature—Should not exceed 11 pounds.

COLOUR
Dachshunds may be any colour other than white, the most commo
being black-and-tan and fawn.

COAT
There are three recognised coats within the breed, all of which appl
alike to Standards and Miniatures. The Smooth carries a short, smoot
dense and strong coat. The Long-Haired dogs have a soft, long coa
often wavy. The Wire-Haired types carry a harsh, short and even coat.

SPECIAL CHARACTERISTICS
The Dachshund is easily recognised by its build, the short legs and pr
portionately long body, being distinctive to the breed. Dachshund
however, must be compact with a well-developed musculature.

USES
Bred originally to hunt badger, the Dachshund is now mainly a pet an
show dog. Their small size makes them an ideal breed for city dwelling.

HISTORY
Although the breed was developed in Germany, little is known of its re
origins. Some writers hold that they spring from the Basset Hound
while others feel that they are a separate breed of great antiquity.

Breed: **DALMATIAN**

ORIGIN Unknown.

SIZE
To 26 inches at the shoulder.
Dogs—55 pounds.
Bitches—50 pounds.

COLOUR
White background colour with spots of either black or liver. The spo[ts]
should be as regular as possible, varying in size from a sixpence to a flori[n]

COAT
Fine and glossy with a sleek quality. To the touch it must be dense an[d]
hard, short in length.

SPECIAL CHARACTERISTICS
Skull flat and broad between ears. Well-defined stop. Head witho[ut]
wrinkle, with a long powerful muzzle. Nose is black with black-spotte[d]
types, liver with liver-spotted. Eyes are wide set, round and intelligent.

USES
A good tracking dog, a better than average retriever. A good obedien[ce]
dog, the Dalmatian has also served with distinction in two World War[s]
They have also been used as herd dogs and can be taught to point.

HISTORY
Although the breed name derives from the Adriatic province of Dalmati[a]
they seem to have existed over much of Europe for many centuries. [A]
favourite of the Gypsies, it is difficult to pinpoint their exact home.

Breed: **DOBERMANN**

ORIGIN Germany.

SIZE
Dogs—25–27 inches at the shoulder.
Bitches—24–26 inches at the shoulder.
Weight is proportionate with maximum of approximately 85 pounds.

COLOUR
Black with tan markings.
Red (brown) with tan markings.
Blue with tan markings.

COAT
Extremely dense but soft coat lying flat.

SPECIAL CHARACTERISTICS
Medium ears, set high. Eyes almond-shaped and dark, nose long, head shaped to resemble a blunt wedge. Tail docked but set high and carried high. Dog gives impression of controlled speed, stamina and tenacity combined with elegance.

USES
Primarily a service dog, the Dobermann is an excellent tracker, saw service on several fronts during World War II. Has been trained as a retriever, a pointer and a herd dog but essentially it is a guard dog.

HISTORY
The only pedigree dog to bear the name of its creator, Louis Dobermann. Dobermann's aim was the setting up of the world's largest terrier.

Breed: **ELKHOUND, NORWEGIAN**

ORIGIN   Norway, Sweden.

SIZE
Dogs—22 inches at the shoulder, 50 pounds.
Bitches—20 inches at the shoulder, 45 pounds.

COLOUR
Grey, with black tips on the long guard hairs.   Background colour is lighter
on chest, stomach, legs and underside of tail.

COAT
A double-coated dog, with the outer coat consisting of thick, rich, harsh
guard-hairs, close growing.   On the head and front of the legs it is quite
short, longest on neck and chest where it may form a positive ruff.

SPECIAL CHARACTERISTICS
Broad headed at the ears, carries a clearly defined stop.   Muzzle is of
medium length, tapers slightly but is not pointed.   Ear set is high, the ear
itself being longer than it is broad at the base and is erect.

USES
A product of the rough Scandinavian terrain, the Elkhound is a hunter
with incredible stamina, capable of following a track for days.   Not as
fast as some hounds, they have been used on a wide variety of game.

HISTORY
One of the large 'Spitz' family, all of whom trace their origins to the
Far North.   Archeological research tends to show that the breed has
existed almost unchanged for nearly eight thousand years.

Breed: **ENGLISH SETTER**

ORIGIN Great Britain (England).

SIZE
Dogs—25–27½ inches at the shoulder, to 66 pounds.
Bitches—24–25½ inches at the shoulder, to 62 pounds.

COLOUR
Black-and-white, liver-and-white, lemon-and-white, blue-and-white, solid white, blue roan or tricolour.

COAT
Long coated, silky with feathering on legs, underside and tail.

SPECIAL CHARACTERISTICS
Head is long, moderately lean with a marked stop. The ears are silky and rounded at the end, of a medium length. The neck is arched, long and lean, without much throat. The tail is set low, reaches only about to the hocks, has a distinct taper. The tail feathering is straight and silky gradually tapering with the tail.

USES
As a gun-dog and as a pet.

HISTORY
Some writers hold that the Setter is the result of careful selective breeding, working with a basic dog known as the 'setting spaniel'. The Setter, they say, is a 'spaniel much improved'. Opposing them is a group which hold the theory true to a point but they insist that the radical 'improvement' was accomplished by crossing Pointers with the Spaniels.

Breed: **FOX-TERRIER, SMOOTH-HAIRED**

ORIGIN   Great Britain (England).

SIZE
15 inches at the shoulder, 18 pounds.
Bitches proportionately smaller.

COLOUR
White is the predominate colour with markings.   Red or liver markings
are considered poor.

COAT
Must be smooth and flat but also hard, abundant and very dense.

SPECIAL CHARACTERISTICS
The Smooth-Haired Fox-Terrier should hold to almost ideal proportions.
With a dog standing 15½ inches at the shoulder, the back should measure
no more than 12 inches from the shoulder to the root of the tail and the
head should be at least 7 inches long.   The dog's movement must be perfectly straight with all the drive coming from the hind legs.

USES
Created to hunt the fox, the Smooth-Haired Fox-Terrier is still capable
of doing his job, may be seen with many hunts today.   Others of the breed
have gained fame as ratters and the breed is excellent against vermin.

HISTORY
The earliest terriers shown in Britain included a class of White and other
Smooth-Haired English Terriers ' so that the Smooth-Haired is one of the
oldest terriers seen in the ring.   It became standardised in 1876.

Breed: FOX-TERRIER, WIRE-HAIRED

ORIGIN   Great Britain (England).

SIZE
15½ inches at the shoulder and weighing about 18 pounds.
Bitches should weigh approximately 2 pounds less.

COLOUR
Predominantly white, with black, tan or grizzle markings, often in the form
of a saddle.

COAT
Hard and wiry as possible, of medium length.   Softness and woolliness are
penalised at exhibitions.

SPECIAL CHARACTERISTICS
A typical terrier in action and behaviour.

USES
Bred for working, the Wire-Haired Fox-Terrier is intelligent, readily adapt-
able and one of the most popular British terriers.   Immaculate and smart
in appearance when trimmed they are good house dogs.

HISTORY
The Wire-Haired Fox-Terrier is older than its cousin the Smooth-Haired.
There is a Dutch painting dated 1748 which shows a dog very similar to
the Wire-Haired Fox-Terrier as it was seen in the early part of the century.
Originally called the Rough-Haired Terrier, the breed was later known as
the White-Haired Terrier and finally received the modern name in 1879.

Breed: **GOLDEN RETRIEVER**

ORIGIN   Russia.

SIZE
   Dogs—23–24 inches at the shoulder, 65 pounds.
   Bitches—20–22 inches at the shoulder, 60 pounds.

COLOUR
   As the name indicates the dogs should be golden in colour. Deeper reds tending towards that of the Irish Setter are frowned on as are light cream colours.

COAT
   The coat may be either flat or wavy but it must be dense and water-resistant and with a good undercoat.

SPECIAL CHARACTERISTICS
   Symmetrically built, active and powerful dogs, Golden Retrievers are noted for their gay expressions. They carry a broad skull and are noted for their intelligence as well as for an extremely acute sense of smell.

USES
   Primarily field dogs, the Golden Retrievers are well thought of for their work in water and have also gained prominence in the field of competitive obedience.

HISTORY
   The breed descends directly from eight Russian Trackers, purchased in 1860 by Sir Dudley Majoribanks. From this foundation stock he created the breed which was first exhibited about 1908 or 1909.

Breed: **GREAT DANE**

ORIGIN   Not definitely known although usually considered to be Germany.

SIZE
Dogs—32 inches at the shoulder.
Bitches—30 inches at the shoulder.
Weight—in proportion to height.

COLOUR
Fawn, brindle, blue, black or harlequin.

COAT
Must be short, thick, smooth and highly glossy.

SPECIAL CHARACTERISTICS
The Great Dane must always give an impression of powerful elegance
combining dignity and strength with size. Weighing over one hundred
pounds in many cases, the Great Dane is one of Britain's largest dogs.

USES
Known as the descendants of the German boar-hounds, Great Dane
probably trace their ancestry much farther back. They are similar to the
Alaunt of the Middle Ages, a dog used on all types of big game. Today
they are used for guard work occasionally and have also adapted them
selves to city life.

HISTORY
Some authorities trace the Great Dane or a very similar dog back t
Egyptian times. Others content themselves with dating the breed i
Grecian sculpture. First shown in Britain in 1877, they were called Boar
hounds in 1882 and were recognised as Great Danes in 1884.

Breed: **GREYHOUND**

ORIGIN   Unknown, possibly Egypt.

SIZE
Dogs—28–30 inches at the shoulder.
Bitches—27–28 inches at the shoulder.
Weight is governed by use to which the dog is put.

COLOUR
Black, white, red, fawn, fallow, brindle or any of the solid colours broke
with white.

COAT
Fine, lying close to the skin.

SPECIAL CHARACTERISTICS
The head is long, with a flat skull and a very slight stop.   The muzzl
tapers and the jaws are extremely powerful.   The eyes are dark an
brilliant, round, set moderately wide.   The tail is set and carried low wit
a slight curve.   The feet are fairly long, with strong, tough pads.

USES
The greyhound is used in Britain for racing or coursing. Some are kept as pet

HISTORY
One of the oldest breeds known to man.   There is one sculpture, date
approximately 2000 B.C. which shows a clearly recognisable smooth
coated greyhound.   The greyhound too is mentioned in the Bible in th
Book of Proverbs.   The breed was found in many parts of the ancien
world, from Greece to Carthage.

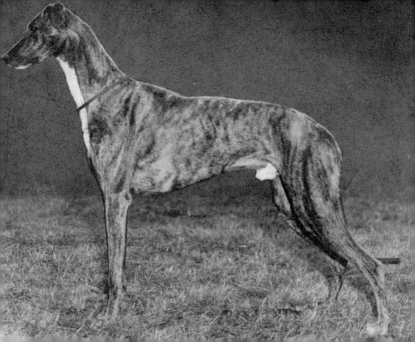

Breed: **GRIFFON BRUXELLOIS**

ORIGIN Belgium.

SIZE
The weight range is from 3–10 pounds.

COLOUR
Red, black or black-and-tan. Technically the black-and-tan is known a
a Belgian Griffon, as is the black. Purists maintain that only the re
is the true Griffon Bruxellois.

COAT
Two coats are seen—the smooth variety being classed as a Brabançon
the wiry coats being Griffons Bruxellois.
Smooth coats are short, dense and smooth, similar to a Boston Terrier.
Wire coats should be dense, harsh to the touch.

SPECIAL CHARACTERISTICS
Skull is rounded and domed. A fringe of whiskers (in the Griffons
Bruxellois) around eyes, nose, cheeks and chin. Ears are small, semi-
erect. Nose black and short, with large nostrils. Stop is pronounced.
The chin is undershot, the lips are edged with black.

USES
As pets and show dogs. Have done remarkably well in competitive
obedience, having a reputation for a high degree of intelligence.

HISTORY
A toy Griffon, native to Belgium, seems to be the foundation stock for
the breed. Later crosses are a matter of guesswork.

Breed: **IRISH SETTER**

ORIGIN   Ireland.

SIZE
Dogs—25 inches at the shoulder, to 60 pounds.
Bitches slightly smaller.

COLOUR
Rich chestnut or mahogany. No black is allowed at exhibitions although
white, in the form of a star or blaze, is permissible.

COAT
On the ear tips, on the head and on the front of the legs, the coat is short
and fine. On the remainder of the body it is of a moderate length, flat
and soft but without wave. Feathering is marked on upper ears, belly,
backs of legs and tail.

SPECIAL CHARACTERISTICS
A lean, racy dog, long bodied, with a characteristically well-furnished coat.
The eyes are a dark hazel and not over-large. The ears, fine and of medium
length hang in a neat fold close to the head. In temperament the breed
is affectionate, tends towards exuberance. Has the best nose of any setter.

USES
As a gun-dog, pet and show dog.

HISTORY
Although the breed is said to originate in Ireland it is probably true that
it evolved there from the same basic stock which also gave rise to the
English and Gordon Setters.

Breed: **IRISH TERRIER**

ORIGIN Great Britain (Ireland) and Eire.

SIZE
18 inches at the shoulder.
Dogs—27 pounds.
Bitches—25 pounds.

COLOUR
Red and wheaten with any intermediate shades.

COAT
Although the coat is broken in appearance it should lie close to the body.
The hairs should grow so closely that if parted by the fingers the skin is
still not visible.   The texture is harsh and wiry.

SPECIAL CHARACTERISTICS
Head is long but in proportion, the skull is flat.   The jaws are described as
' punishing '.   The nose must be black.   Eyes are dark hazel, small, fiery
and intelligent.   Ears are small, moderately thick and V-shaped, dropping
forward along the cheeks.

USES
The breed developed along lines which enabled it to play an active part
in vermin hunting in its native Ireland.   They are superb house dogs.

HISTORY
Although the breed is counted as having originated in Ireland, it seems
that, like the Airedale and the Welsh Terrier, they owe much to the wire-
haired black-and-tan working terrier of two centuries ago.

Breed: **IRISH WOLF HOUND**

ORIGIN   Great Britain (Ireland).

SIZE
Dogs—32 inches at the shoulder, 120 pounds (minimum).
Bitches—30 inches at the shoulder, 105 pounds (minimum).

COLOUR
Black, white, fawn, red, grey or brindle.

COAT
Rough, harsh body hair, growing longer over eyes and under the jaw.

SPECIAL CHARACTERISTICS
A big dog, with a long moderately wide skull and a long muzzle. The
ears are comparatively small and resemble those of a greyhound. The tail
is long and curves slightly and should be well covered with hair. The feet
are large and round, the toes close together. The back is short and
should arch over the loins.

USES
A companion, guard and pet in Britain, the Irish Wolf Hound is used
abroad as a coursing hunter, capable of killing a wolf single-handed.

HISTORY
Irish Wolf Hounds were shipped from the British Isles to Imperial Rome
as early as A.D. 391 when ' All Rome viewed them with wonder '. The breed
began to disappear when their natural prey the wolf became extinct and
today's animals are the result of a careful breeding programme undertaken
in the last century. Then, Captain G. A. Graham recreated these, the
largest dogs in the world.

Breed: **KEESHOND**

ORIGIN Holland.

SIZE
Dogs—18 inches at the shoulder.
Bitches—17 inches at the shoulder.

COLOUR
Wolf grey or ash grey, the markings distinct against body colour. Neve
all white or all black.

COAT
Carries a dense soft, thick undercoat which is a lighter colour than the
outer coat, which is dense, profuse, harsh to touch and standing out from
body. A definite ruff must be carried, the legs are trousered in fur.

SPECIAL CHARACTERISTICS
Wedge-shaped head, proportionate to the body. There is a definite stop.
The eyes are dark and have fully marked 'spectacles', the absence of
which shows incorrect breeding. The ears are small, well-furred and erect.
The tail curls tightly and in some cases may form a double curl. It is tipped
with black but the top of the curve is white. Feet are small and cat-like.

USES
A pet, companion and show dog. In their native Holland they are used as
barge-dogs, protecting their masters' craft.

HISTORY
One of the Spitz family, the Keeshond is reputed by many to be the
ancestor of the Pomeranian. The breed was introduced in Britain in 1900.

Breed: **LABRADOR RETRIEVER**

ORIGIN   Great Britain, via Newfoundland and Labrador.

SIZE
Dogs—22–24 inches at the shoulder, 75 pounds in weight.
Bitches—1 inch shorter than dogs, 5 pounds lighter in weight.

COLOUR
Solid black or solid yellow.

COAT
Short and dense but without any wave.   Harsh to the hand.   There shoul
be no feathering.

SPECIAL CHARACTERISTICS
The Labrador Retriever is a strong dog, short coupled but extremely active
Wide over the loins, the hind-quarters must be strong and muscula
The skull is wide.

USES
Without a doubt the most popular retriever both in Britain and in th
United States.   Used extensively both in the field and in water.

HISTORY
The first recorded Labradors appear in Britain in 1835 although the bree
may have existed previously.   They were then known as Newfoundlan
dogs but later took the Labrador name.   They were, apparently, descend
ants of dogs taken to the New World by fishermen almost two centurie
previously and are thus British in origin.   The breed was recognised a
such by the Kennel Club in 1903.

Breed: **LAKELAND TERRIER**

ORIGIN   Great Britain (England).

SIZE
Up to 16 pounds, with the dogs' average height about 14½ inches.

COLOUR
A variety of colours are recognised—among them black-and-tan, blue-and-tan, wheaten, red and grizzle-red.

COAT
The coat is harsh, dense and wiry, offering complete resistance to the weather. On the legs the hair is longer, as it is on the face and jaws.

SPECIAL CHARACTERISTICS
Ears are small, set on the side of the head rather than the top, they are V-shaped and must be carried at the alert. Eyes are small, dark and no prominent.

USES
Although Lakeland Terriers are often seen today in the show ring they were bred for work and are still used for vermin hunting in many parts of the country. They have also been used as herd and guard dogs.

HISTORY
Bred in and around the Cumberland Fells, the Lakeland is closely akin to the Border Terrier, the Dandie Dinmount Terrier and the Bedlington Terrier. First shown before World War I the breed was not officially named or a standard drawn up until 1921.

Breed: **MALTESE**

ORIGIN   Unknown.

SIZE
Not to exceed 9 pounds.   The smaller the better.

COLOUR
White.

COAT
Long, straight, silky and strong.   No undercoat.   In adult dogs the co
parts down the spine, drops on either side.

SPECIAL CHARACTERISTICS
Head fine and with a slightly rounded skull.   Ears set slightly low, wi
profuse feathering.   Eyes are dark with an alert gentle expression, bla
eyelids.   Nose is black as are the pads of the feet.   Tail is well feathere
carried gracefully with the tip resting on the hind-quarters.

USES
As pets and companions, or as show dogs.

HISTORY
One of the oldest known lap dogs, the Maltese were described by Strab
saying ' they were accounted the jewels of women . . .'   Although it
often assumed that the breed came from the island of Malta there is litt
proof of this and some of the first of these animals to arrive here came fro
Manila in the Philippines.   Despite this, there appear to have been Malte
in England at least two hundred years ago.   Possibly the breed originate
in and around Melita in Sicily, the name being corrupted to Malta.

Breed: **NEWFOUNDLAND**

ORIGIN Newfoundland.

SIZE
Dogs—28 inches at the shoulder, to 150 pounds.
Bitches—26 inches at the shoulder, to 120 pounds.

COLOUR
All black or parti-coloured (Landseers). The parti-colours may be of any hue but the preference is for black-and-white, or bronze-and-white.

COAT
Flat, very thick and of a distinct oily texture. Must shed and resist water

SPECIAL CHARACTERISTICS
Head broad and massive. Little stop, muzzle short, clean cut and square in shape. The eyes are small, usually dark brown, set deeply and wide apart with no haw showing. Ears are small, set well back close to the head and completely covered with short hair. The tail is medium length and reaching down to the hocks, well covered with hair but not feathered. In normal circumstances it hangs down but when the dog is excited it is carried straight with a slight curve.

USES
As a pet, companion or show dog.

HISTORY
The origin of the breed is not quite clear but it reached its peak of development in England. Over a century ago the Newfoundland dogs were much smaller than they are today.

Breed: NORWICH TERRIER

ORIGIN   Great Britain (England).

SIZE
11 pounds is ideal weight, with an average height of 10 inches.

COLOUR
Red, wheaten, black-and-tan or brindle.

COAT
The coat should be hard and wiry with no softness or silkiness.   During winter the coat grows longer so that the dogs have a partial mane about the shoulders and neck.   One of the few breeds in which trimming or stripping may be penalised at exhibitions.

SPECIAL CHARACTERISTICS
The Norwich Terrier has a small neat ear which may be either pricked or dropped.   The eyes are dark, keen and bright.   The skull is wide slightly rounded and with a good span between the eyes.

USES
Created approximately one hundred years ago primarily as ratters, the Norwich Terriers may still be used for ratting but they are essentially pets and companions.

HISTORY
Based probably on Irish Terrier foundations, the Norwich is presumed also to have crosses of Border Terriers, Staffordshires and possibly Bedlingtons.   At one time several strains existed, only one of which was known as the Norwich.

Breed: **PAPILLON**

ORIGIN Belgium.

SIZE
From 3–6 pounds.

COLOUR
White with black or brown markings, tricolour.

COAT
Dense coat of soft, silky texture. Coat is short on the muzzle, head and forepart of legs. Otherwise it is longish with a great deal of feathering.

SPECIAL CHARACTERISTICS
Two types are recognised—one with drop ears, the other with obliquely set and upright ears, which give the dogs the popular name of 'Butterfly Dogs'. The tail, which is quite bushy and carried high, has given the breed still another name, for in France they are called 'Squirrel Dogs'. The feet of the Papillon may have fine tufts of hair growing up between the toes but they should not make the foot heavy.

USES
As a pet and show dog.

HISTORY
Some people believe that the Papillon is directly related to the Chihuahua, and that it was imported from Mexico. There is considerable doubt about this idea though and most authorities agree that the breed is the result of a mutation on the old Belgian Toy Spaniel. In some places the drop-eared Papillons are still classed as such.

Breed: **PEKINGESE**

ORIGIN China.

SIZE
Dogs—up to 12 pounds.
Bitches—in proportion.

COLOUR
Pekingese can be any colour except albino and liver. If the background colour is broken or marked, the breaking should be even and as symmetrical as possible.

COAT
Long and straight, rather coarse to the touch. The undercoat is thick and dense. The outer coat must form a mane or cape round the neck. There is feathering around ears, legs, toes and tail.

SPECIAL CHARACTERISTICS
The dog should show in its expression, evidence of its Oriental origin. The skull is massive, wide and flat between the ears. The eyes are large and dark, tending to be prominent. The stop is deep and the nose, which is black must be short and flat. The ears are heart shaped, set moderately low with a long feather. The tail is set high, is carried well over the back.

USES
Watch dogs of exceptional intelligence and extremely high spirits. Excellent pets and companions.

HISTORY
An extremely old breed they were reserved, in their homeland, for royalty

Breed: **POINTER**

ORIGIN Spain.

SIZE
Up to 24 inches at the shoulder, top weight about 55–60 pounds.

COLOUR
Black-and-white, lemon-and-white, orange-and-white, liver-and-white, solid colours and tricolours.

COAT
Short and smooth to the touch but hard. Straight, lying close to the body and with a decided sheen or gloss.

SPECIAL CHARACTERISTICS
Symmetry is one of the most desirable qualities in the pointer. It must balance all round to be of top quality. The skull is long, moderately wide with a marked stop. The muzzle is long, square and straight allowing adequate space for the mechanism of scenting. No matter what the colour of the dog, dark eyes are desirable, and the ears which are thin should hang just below the throat.

USES
As a gun-dog or pet.

HISTORY
The breed is generally conceded to be Spanish in origin although similar dogs were known in many parts of Europe, notably France and Belgium where they were known as *bracques*. The breed as we know it today was developed in England by careful selective breeding.

Breed: **POMERANIAN**

ORIGIN Germany—and other sections of Europe.

SIZE
Should not exceed 7 pounds.

COLOUR
White, black, brown, blue, orange, beaver or any other self-colour. Ther
should be no white or black shadings.

COAT
Coat is massive. Top coat long, straight, harsh. Coat forms a ma
around chest and shoulders. Feathering on hind-quarters down to hock
Tail has long spreading hair.   Undercoat is soft, fluffy and dense.

SPECIAL CHARACTERISTICS
Head is small, with smooth hair and a fox-like appearance. Ears a
carried erect. The tail characteristically curls back over the body. Sku
is flat and large in proportion to the very fine muzzle. Eyes are mediu
sized, set obliquely and dark in colour. In white dogs the eyelids shou
be black. In blacks and browns the nose is self-coloured, in all oth
types it should be black.

USES
As a pet and show dog.

HISTORY
One of the Spitz family, the Pomeranian derives its name from one sectio
of Germany. Up until the turn of the century the breed was much large

Breed: **POODLE (Standard, Miniature and Toy)**

ORIGIN Germany.

SIZE
Standard—15 inches and over at the shoulder.
Miniature—Under 15 inches at the shoulder.
Toy—Under 11 inches at the shoulder.

COLOUR
Black, white, brown, blue or any solid colour. Parti-colour poodles occur
but are not eligible for exhibition.

COAT
A dense, profuse coat with a hard texture. When pressed by the hand it
should instantly spring back into position. Unlike many long-haired
dogs the poodle sheds little.

SPECIAL CHARACTERISTICS
Extremely active yet elegant dogs. Built well and proportionately. Should
have a proud carriage and possess exceptional intelligence.

USES
Originally a working retriever, whose thick coat gave it great protection
against icy water. Now primarily a pet or show dog. The three types
differ essentially only in size.

HISTORY
Brought by German troops into France, the poodle was long called the
national dog of France. For many years the breed was a favourite in
circuses. Today the two smaller types are the world's most popular dogs.

Breed: **PUG**

ORIGIN China.

SIZE
Between 14 and 18 pounds, the smaller being preferable.

COLOUR
Silver, apricot, fawn or black.

COAT
Fine and smooth, soft to the touch, thick and glossy.

SPECIAL CHARACTERISTICS
Square, compact dogs, well muscled and cobby. Rib development is sufficient to give a very wide chest. Head is massive and rounded. The muzzle is short and extremely blunt. Eyes which are dark are extremely prominent. Ears are thin and soft, feel like velvet to the touch. The tail curls round over the back, may sometimes achieve a complete double curve.

USES
As pets, companions and show dogs.

HISTORY
The breed was long thought to be Dutch but modern research has proved that the original Pugs were brought to Holland from China. The first Pugs came to Britain in the first half of the last century and the breed became very popular until about 1900. Many years ago the Pug was chosen as the symbol of the Orange Party in Dutch politics, in opposition to the Keeshond which was the mascot of the other party.

Breed: **PYRENEAN MOUNTAIN DOG**

ORIGIN   France.

SIZE
Dogs—27–32 inches at shoulder, to 125 pounds.
Bitches—25–29 inches at the shoulder, to 115 pounds.
Length, from shoulder blades to tail root should correspond to height at shoulder.

COLOUR
Pure white, or white with badger, grey or tan markings.

COAT
Double coated.   Undercoat is fine, close lying and white.   The outer coat is long, flat and thick.   It may be straight or slightly waved.

SPECIAL CHARACTERISTICS
Skull large, wedge-shaped.   Little or no stop.   Head has been compared with that of a brown bear in basic structure.   Eyes are set obliquely, are dark brown and of medium size.   Ears are V-shaped, with rounded tips, set on parallel with eyes.   Tail long enough to reach below hocks, carried low normally, high when alert.   Plumed or feathered.

USES
As a guard or watch dog, pet or show specimen.   Still used as a herd guard in its native France.

HISTORY
Thought to be a direct descendant of the ancient Asiatic mastiffs.   Once the Royal Dogs of France, they are mentioned as early as 1407.

Breed: **ST. BERNARD**

ORIGIN Switzerland.

SIZE
The bigger the dog, the better it is, provided that it maintains good proportion and symmetry. Some specimens of the breed have reached a weight of more than 200 pounds.

COLOUR
Mahogany brindle, red brindle, orange or white with patches of the listed self-colours. Where markings occur they should be as follows—white muzzle with an additional streak of white up the face. A white collar running around the neck and connecting with a white chest. The fore legs, feet and end of the tail should also be white.

COAT
Rough—a dense, flat coat gradually becoming fuller around the neck. Smooth—the coat is similar to that of a hound.

SPECIAL CHARACTERISTICS
A massive head, the skull slightly rounded, giving a prominent brow. Muzzle is short and square at the nose. The stop is abrupt, the nose straight and quite broad. Nose black, the eyes small.

USES
Sledge dog, guide, companion, show dog.

HISTORY
Developed to work in the Swiss Alps, it appears to have descended from the now extinct Alpine Mastiff.

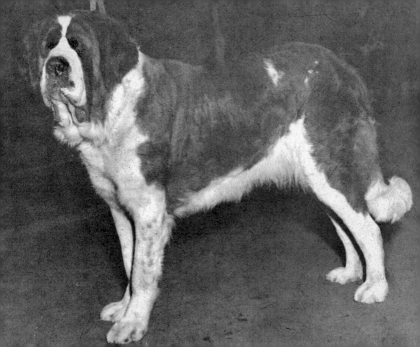

Breed: **SAMOYED**

ORIGIN Asia (Siberia).

SIZE
Dogs—20–22 inches at the shoulder, 50–55 pounds.
Bitches—18–20 inches at the shoulder, 38–45 pounds.

COLOUR
White, cream or white-and-biscuit.

COAT
The body is completely covered with a dense, soft, short undercoat, through which the guard hairs, which form the outer coat, grow. These guard hairs are harsh and stand straight out from the body.

SPECIAL CHARACTERISTICS
Powerful wedge-shaped head with a flat, broad skull. The muzzle is medium, the front of the face tapering. Lips are black, nose should be black. The eyes, set wide apart and deep, are dark with an alert look. The ears are medium length, with rounded tips, set well apart.

USES
Bred in Siberia by the Samoyed tribes, the breed was used originally for guarding reindeer herds and for pulling sledges. They have since distinguished themselves as sledge dogs in both the Arctic and Antarctic.

HISTORY
Part of the Spitz family, the breed was isolated for centuries until the heyday of Arctic exploration. Since then, specimens have been brought into the outside world and have gained wide acceptance as pets.

Breed: **SCHNAUZER, MINIATURE**

ORIGIN Germany.

SIZE

Dogs—14 inches at the shoulder.
Bitches—13 inches at the shoulder.
Above 14 inches the dogs are disqualified from exhibitions.

COLOUR

Any combination of salt-and-pepper or a solid black.

COAT

Hard and wiry, not smooth or too long but slightly rough in appearance.
The outer coat is harsh to the hand, the undercoat close and soft.

SPECIAL CHARACTERISTICS

The skull is moderately broad, muzzle strong for its size, with a blunt end
and furnished with wiry whiskers. The eyes are medium sized, oval in
shape and dark brown. The tip of the nose is black. The ears are small,
V-shaped, folding forward to lie close to the skull. The tail, carried erect
and set high should be no longer than one inch.

USE

House guard and ratter. Distinct terrier-like qualities.

HISTORY

Derives from the Standard Schnauzer, which is slightly larger than the
Miniature. It seems to be the result of outcrossing the Standard with the
Affenpinscher. In Germany the Miniature Schnauzer is widely used as
a ratter, particularly to keep it a ' working dog ' as opposed to a pure
' show dog '.

Breed: **SCOTTISH TERRIER**

ORIGIN   Great Britain (Scotland).

SIZE
Both sexes height at the shoulder about 10 inches.
Dogs up to 22 pounds.
Bitches up to 20 pounds.

COLOUR
Black, wheaten or brindled.
A short, wiry coat, maximum length about 2 inches.   The undercoat is dense, while the outer coat is harsh to the touch.

SPECIAL CHARACTERISTICS
Head and tail should be carried well up, the animal giving an appearance of keenness, sharpness and activeness.   Despite its small size the Scottish Terrier should always be heavily muscled.

USES
The result of cross-breeding among various types of older terriers, the Scottish breed was designed for use against rats and other pests. Most of today's Scottish Terriers are seen in the show ring but they will still tackle anything, being totally fearless.

HISTORY
Several other types of terrier were once called Scottish Terriers but apparently the foundation stock from which the British derive these dogs came from Perthshire and from the Moor of Rannoch. The standard for the breed was drawn up in 1880 and a breed club established two years later.

Breed: **SEALYHAM TERRIER**

ORIGIN   Great Britain (Wales).

SIZE
About 10 inches at the shoulder with a body weight of 18–20 pounds.

COLOUR
All white, or white with lemon, tan or badger markings on the head. Markings should not be heavy.

COAT
A soft, dense undercoat topped by a harsh, wiry outer coat. Soft or silky coats are not desirable.

SPECIAL CHARACTERISTICS
The hind-legs are slightly longer than the fore-legs but the top line is still flat. The length of the back from the shoulder to the tail set should be approximately that of the dog's height so that he is roughly square. The eyes are dark, wide set and oval, with a typical terrier expression. The nose should be black.

USES
Bred as a vermin hunter, the Sealyham is still used for that purpose. Despite this, they make excellent pets and are growing more and more popular.

HISTORY
The Sealyham Terrier was created by Captain John Edwardes from Pembrokeshire Corgis, Dandie Dinmounts, West Highland Whites and perhaps the Bull Terrier. Recognised by the Kennel Club in 1911.

Breed: **SHETLAND SHEEPDOG**

ORIGIN   Great Britain (Shetland Isles).

SIZE
Best height is 14 inches at the shoulder.

COLOUR
Tricolour (black-and-tan with white), black-and-white, sable, sable-and-white, blue merle and blue merle-and-white.

COAT
Double-coated with a harsh long, straight outer coat. The undercoat grows close, is short and furry. Mane is abundant and the fore-legs are feathered. The face is smooth.

SPECIAL CHARACTERISTICS
Flat skull, tapering in width from ears towards eyes. Very little stop, muzzle of moderate length. Eyes medium, almond-shaped and dark (merles sometimes have blue eyes). Ears small, wide at base, carried semi-erect when dog is excited.

USES
Bred originally to work with both sheep and cattle, the Shetland Sheepdogs retain their basic abilities but are more often seen as pets and show dogs.

HISTORY
Crofters on the islands brought in small Rough Collies, bred from them to achieve the Shetland Sheepdog. There was probably some Icelandic Dog added to the breed, which was finally set by judicious additions of more Rough Collie blood.

Breed: **SHIZTZU**

ORIGIN Tibet.

SIZE

Up to $10\frac{1}{2}$ inches at the shoulder with weight varying between 13 and 1 pounds.

COLOUR

Any colour can occur; a white blaze on the forehead and a white tail-ti are highly prized. Liver marked dogs are allowed to have lighter eyes tha other colours.

COAT

Outer coat is long and dense but without curl. Undercoat is thick, an woolly.

SPECIAL CHARACTERISTICS

Skull is broad and round with wide spacing between eyes. Muzzle square and short, flat and quite hairy. Nose should be black, separate from stop by about one inch. Hair on nose grows upward to give chrys anthemum effect. Whiskers and beard are prominent. The eyes are roun dark and large but not prominent. Ears are large and drooping, set belo crown of skull.

USES

House dog or guard, pet or companion.

HISTORY

One of the Tibetan breeds, the Shiztzu was used in its home as a guar since it is utterly fearless. First introduced into Britain about thirty year ago it was known as the Tibetan Lion Dog but the name was later change

Breed: **SPRINGER SPANIEL (English)**

ORIGIN Great Britain (England).

SIZE

Dogs—To 20 inches at the shoulder and 50 pounds.
Bitches—Proportionately smaller.

COLOUR

Liver-and-white, liver-and-tan, black-and-tan, black-and-white, tan-and-white, roan, black. Red is not a desirable colour.

COAT

On the head, fronts of legs, the hair is short and fine. On the remainder o the body it is medium length and flat, giving, through density, complete resistance to water, weather and thorns. Ideally there should be a fring on the throat, brisket, chest and belly.

SPECIAL CHARACTERISTICS

Head is medium length, moderately broad, with a clear stop and a strong lean jaw. Eyes are of medium size and should harmonise with coat althougl a dark eye is always preferable. The ears, long and lobular, are set on the head no higher than a line extending backward from the eyes.

USES

As a gun-dog, pet, companion or show dog.

HISTORY

Like all spaniels, the English Springer Spaniel is probably Spanish i origin. Once one of the so-called Land Spaniels, the Springer derive its name from the fact that it was used to spring or flush its game for nets falcons, hounds and later, guns.

Breed: **STAFFORDSHIRE BULL TERRIER**

ORIGIN   Great Britain (England).

SIZE
> 14–16 inches at the shoulder.
> Dogs—To 38 pounds.
> Bitches—To 34 pounds.

COLOUR
> Black, blue, fawn, red, white, brindle, brindle-and-white or any of th
> self-colours marked with white.

COAT
> Short and close, stiff and hard to the touch but glossy.

SPECIAL CHARACTERISTICS
> Head and skull short and broad, black nosed.   Ears rose-shaped or hal
> pricked.   The face has a distinct stop and the eyes are set so as to look dea
> ahead.   Cheek muscles are pronounced and the front of the face is rathe
> short.   The legs, set wide apart are heavily boned and straight.   The bod
> is lightly loined in comparison with the barrel-like rib spring.

USES
> House dogs, guards, pets, companions and show dogs.

HISTORY
> Opinion varies as to the source of the Staffordshire Bull Terrier.   Som
> authorities feel that this is the direct descendent of the old Bull-and-Terrie
> which in turn was a cross derived from the fighting Bulldog and the old blacl
> and-tan wire-haired terrier.   Others claim a more mixed ancestry.

Breed: **WELSH TERRIER**

ORIGIN Great Britain (Wales).

SIZE
15 inches at the shoulder, 20 pounds, with the bitches slightly smaller.

COLOUR
Black-and-tan or dark grizzle and tan.

COAT
A close abundant coat, wiry and harsh to the touch.

SPECIAL CHARACTERISTICS
In silhouette, the Welsh Terrier is almost identical to the Wire-Haired Fox-Terrier. The ears are V-shaped, small, set quite high and carried forward on the cheeks. Eyes are small, quite dark and with an alert look.

USES
Bred for work, the Welsh Terriers, excellent ratters, are used often to draw badger.

HISTORY
Originally called the ' Welsh ' or ' Old English Wire-Haired Black-and-Tan Terrier ', the breed gained its modern name in 1888. The Welsh Terrier then is a representative of the breed which played a large part in the foundation of many of the British modern terriers, including the Airedale. Oddly, although the breed is gay and companionable it has never achieved much popularity either in Britain or abroad. One interesting point in the breed history occurred when a well-known specimen proved to be the result of a cross between a Wire-Haired Fox-Terrier and an Airedale Terrier.

Breed: **WEST HIGHLAND WHITE TERRIER**

ORIGIN   Great Britain (Scotland).

SIZE
Dogs—10–12 inches at the shoulder, 15–19 pounds.
Bitches—8–10 inches at the shoulder, 13–17 pounds.

COLOUR
Pure white only.

COAT
Double-coated.   Outer coat must be harsh and free from curl.   Undercoat is like a fur, short, close and soft.

SPECIAL CHARACTERISTICS
The roof of the mouth is often black, as are the pads.   The tail should be carried erect but not over the back.   If the tail is more than 6 inches long the dog may be penalised at exhibitions.   General appearance is typical of the terrier group.

USES
First used on small game and vermin, the West Highland White Terrier will still pursue prey without thought of quitting.   Moderately popular as pets they are still primarily workers although they are classified as Terriers.

HISTORY
Developing from the same background as the Scottish Terriers, the Cairn Terriers and the Dandie Dinmount Terriers, the West Highlands were set by using white puppies.   At one time known as Poltallochs they were also called White Scottish Terriers before the present name was finally adopted.

Breed: **WHIPPET**

ORIGIN   Great Britain (England).

SIZE
Dogs—18½ inches at the shoulder.
Bitches—17½ inches at the shoulder.
Weight should be proportionate.

COLOUR
Any colour or combination of colours is allowed.

COAT
Smooth, close-lying and firm in texture.

SPECIAL CHARACTERISTICS
The Whippet is essentially a miniature of the Greyhound. It carries a lon
lean head, black nosed with a barely perceptible stop. The muzzle must b
powerful without at the same time showing any coarseness. The eyes ar
bright and intelligent, with yellow or oblique eyes penalised. Feet ar
strong and cat-like.

USES
Bred for rabbit hunting, the Whippet is a 'chaser', working by sight like
his large cousin the Greyhound. In the United States Whippets are often
raced on tracks; here they are common as show dogs.

HISTORY
The record of the origin of the Whippet is confused, the concensus o
opinion being that it is the result of crossing the Italian Greyhound wit
some form of terrier. No matter what its origins or background, th
Whippet is today a miniature of the Greyhound.

Breed: **YORKSHIRE TERRIER**

ORIGIN   Great Britain (England).

SIZE
Up to 7 pounds but since this is a toy breed, the smaller animals are give
preference.

COLOUR
Steel blue along the back, from the back of the skull to the base of the ta
The tail itself should be of a darker blue, while the remainder of the bo
should be a rich, red tan.

COAT
The coat of the Yorkshire Terrier is one of its most important points a
must be long and perfectly straight, with a silky gloss. In the tan areas t
colour must be graduated with the darker colour at the base of the ha
lighter in the middle and lightest at the tips.

SPECIAL CHARACTERISTICS
V-shaped ears which are carried erect or semi-erect. Body is tight-k
and compact. The feet should be round, the toe nails black. The ta
with its blue pluming is carried a little above the level of the back.

USES
As pets, companions and show dogs. There have in addition been instanc
when Yorkshire Terriers have proven their worth as ratters.

HISTORY
Created approximately one hundred years ago. The background probab
carries a variety of small terrier and toy dog bloods.

INDEX